Katie Woo's Hilarious Holiday Jokes

Based on characters created by Fran Manushkin

edited by Blake Hoena

illustrated by Tammie Lyon

PICTURE WINDOW BOOKS
a capstone imprint

Katie Woo is published by Picture Window Books,
A Capstone Imprint
1710 Roe Crest Drive
North Mankato, Minnesota 56003
www.mycapstone.com

Cataloging-in-Publication Data is available on the Library of Congress website.

ISBN: 978-1-5158-0972-2 (library binding)
ISBN: 978-1-5158-0976-0 (paperback)
ISBN: 978-1-5158-0988-3 (eBook PDF)

Summary: Make this collection of laughs part of your holiday traditions. Katie Woo and her friends can't wait to make you giggle with this collection of holiday-themed jokes. Also included are tips on how to tell a joke, sure to make you the funniest person at the party.

Designer: Kayla Dohmen

Printed in the United States of America.
00xxxxxxx

Table of Contents

Mushy, Gushy VALENTINE'S DAY Jokes

What did one rowboat say to the other rowboat?

"Are you ready for a little ROW-mance?"

What do you call two birds in love?

TWEET-hearts.

Knock, knock. Who's there?

Olive. Olive who?

Olive you!

What did the candy tell its sweetheart?

"We're MINT for each other."

What did the paperclip say to the magnet?

"I'm attracted to you."

What did the rabbit say to its sweetheart?

"Some-BUNNY loves you."

Hippity, Hoppity
EASTER
Jokes

What do you call a funny Easter egg?

A practical YOLKER!

What did the rabbit say to the carrot?

"It's been nice GNAWING you!"

Knock, knock. Who's there?
Egg. Egg who?
Are you EGG-cited to see me?

Why couldn't the Easter egg cross the road?

Because it wasn't a chicken yet.

Why did the Easter egg hide?

It was a little chicken.

Why shouldn't you tell an Easter egg a joke?

It gets all cracked up.

How does the Easter bunny stay healthy and strong?

By EGGS-ercising.

Booming
INDEPENDENCE DAY
Jokes

**What do you get when
you cross fireworks
with a duck?**

A fire-QUACKER!

**What's the difference between
a duck and George Washington?**

One has a bill on his face,
the other, his face on a bill.

What's red, white, and blue?

A sad candy cane.

Why did JoJo wear her striped shirt to the 4th of July Picnic?

Because she didn't want to be spotted.

What did one flag say to the other flag?

Nothing. It just waved.

What did Katie Woo draw for her 4th of July art project?

A Yankee Doodle.

Miss Winkle: Can anyone tell me where the Declaration of Independence was signed?

Katie: At the bottom, Miss Winkle.

Chilling, Thrilling
HALLOWEEN
Jokes

Why was the jack-o'-lantern so afraid all the time?

It had no guts.

What did the pumpkin dress up as for Halloween?

An orange.

Who is the funniest monster around?

PRANK-enstein.

How do you fix a broken jack-o'-lantern?

With a pumpkin patch.

How do you make a werewolf laugh?

Let him eat your funny bone.

What is a witch's favorite subject in school?

SPELL-ing.

Why did the zombie stay home from school?

He felt rotten.

What do ghosts wear for Halloween?

BOO jeans.

Knock, knock.

Who's there?

Interrupting ghost.

Interrupt—

BOO!

Which monster is the best dancer?

The boogie-man.

Katie: How many monsters does it take to change a light bulb?
JoJo: I don't know. How many?
Katie: I don't know either. I was too afraid to stay and find out.

What did the vampire say to his girlfriend?

"It was love at first BITE!"

What is the ghost's favorite ride at the fair?

The SCARY-go-round.

JoJo: I heard you have a monster in your closet.
Katie: Yeah, he picked out this outfit for me.

Tummy Rumbling
THANKSGIVING
Jokes

Why didn't the turkey come to Thanksgiving dinner?

It was already stuffed.

Why did the Pilgrim's pants fall down?

Because he wore his belt buckle on his hat.

Why did the turkey cross the road?

It was the chicken's day off.

**What type of key can't
open doors?**

A tur-KEY.

**What do you get when you
sit on a pumpkin?**

A squash.

**Why did the farmer use
sugar to fertilize his crops?**

He wanted to grow sweet potatoes.

**If April showers bring May flowers,
what do Mayflowers bring?**

Pilgrims.

Knock, knock.
Who's there?
Harry.
Harry who?
Harry up with Thanksgiving dinner. I'm hungry!

What sound does a turkey's phone make?

WING, WING!

Knock, knock. Who's there?
Arthur. Arthur who?
Arthur any leftovers from Thanksgiving dinner?

Very Merry CHRISTMAS Jokes

What do the elves do after school?

Their GNOME-work.

What did people call Santa after he lost all of his money?

Saint Nickle-less.

How did the snowman get to school?

By riding an ICICLE.

What do you get when you cross a snowman with a dog?

Frostbite.

What did the snowman eat for breakfast?

Snowflakes.

Knock, knock. Who's there?
Olive. Olive who?
Olive the other reindeer!

What do you call Santa's cat?

Santa CLAWS.

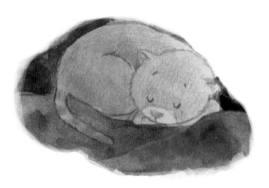

Knock, knock. Who's there?
Emma. Emma who?
Emma going to get lots of presents for Christmas!

HOW TO TELL A JOKE

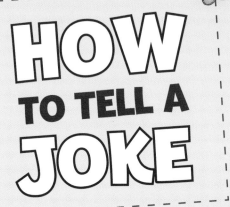

Even the funniest jokes can get groans if you don't tell them right. Here are my best joke-telling tips!

Know your audience— Everybody has a different sense of humor. That means different things make different people laugh. My friends like jokes about school and gross things. My grandparents think jokes about old stuff are a hoot. So I pick jokes that my audience is sure to laugh at.

by Katie Woo

Know your material—I memorize my jokes. I like to stand in front of a mirror and practice the joke until I know it by heart. That way I know I'll do a good job when I'm ready to tell it to someone.

Timing—Most jokes have two parts. The setup says what the joke is about, and the punch line is the funny part. Here's an example:

Setup: What did the pumpkin dress up as for Halloween?
Punch line: An orange.

After I say the setup, I'm always excited to blurt out the punch line right away. But I stop myself. Instead, I take a deep breath and slowly count "one-banana, two-banana" in my head. That way my audience has time to think about the joke. If they don't answer by two-banana, then I shout the punch line. Ha!

Katie Woo's
stories keep the laughs going!

Katie Woo, Super Scout

Katie's Happy Mother's Day

Katie's Noisy Music

Katie's Spooky Sleepover

THE FUN DOESN'T STOP HERE!

Discover more at www.capstonekids.com

- Videos & Contests
- Games & Puzzles
- Friends & Favorites
- Authors & Illustrators

Find cool websites and more books like this one at www.facthound.com.
Just type in the Book ID:
9781515809722
and you're ready to go!